# UNSTABLE TIME

❖

# PATRICIA BYRNE

Belfast
LAPWING

First Published by Lapwing Publications
c/o 1, Ballysillan Drive
Belfast BT14 8HQ
lapwing.poetry@ntlworld.com
http://www.freewebs.com/lapwingpoetry/

Since before 1632
The Greig sept of the MacGregor Clan
Has been printing and binding books

All Lapwing Publications are
Hand-printed and Hand-bound in Belfast
Set in Aldine 721 BT at the Winepress

ISBN 978-1-907276-17-0

# CONTENTS

# ACKNOWLEDGEMENTS

Thanks to the editors of the following in which some of these
poems previously appeared:

The Stony Thursday Book,
Southword,
Moloch,
Sharp Review,
ROPES,
Revival,
First Edition (UK),
Virtual Writer,
Cathach and Swarthmore Literary Review (USA).

# UNSTABLE TIME

# RED RAW

## RED RAW

The sow paws and kicks dry straw,
snorting hot fumes, heavy hanging
milk-blown udder,
gorged teats.

*There, there, that's my girl*, he soothes.

Flanks sink, she kneels,
he rubs her belly snaking round,
bristle sounds like shaving stubble,
scratching roughness.

She settles, he arranges
udder and teats on prickly straw,
then moves to pull the bloodied,
slimy creature from her,
cord breaking.

He forces air passages,
straw-dries oily mucus,
takes pliers and cracks teeth,
then lifts and lays to mother's teat.

Outside, the brown-ringed haloed moon
oozes creamy light on a red-raw
chink of dawn.

## EVENING

A robin flits across the hawthorn
spilling petals like snowflakes

on fern, buttercup and nettle.
The petals bleed

pink at the edges and soon
the bush will turn a milky red

outshone by the elderflower beneath
before May is gone.

The hawthorn is mirrored
in her death-room window

near where midges hover
in the evening sun.

Floating memories
of first menstrual blood
on calico.

## MAMMISI WOMAN

At Turlough
the new-born heifer-calf wobbles
on bruised legs as a pigeon perches
on the galvanised roof.
Gorse blazes through the barn opening
in a sweet whiff of afterbirth.

Next morning I fly to Egypt
and soon watch palm tree shadows
on Nile mud banks like cotton stains.
Images of Hathor cow goddess
at Luxor Temple in the Valley of Kings
where orange acacia blooms
sparrow droppings soil the hieroglyphics
and a Mammisi woman strides
a birth stool.

Once more I am bruised
and birth torn.

# GRANDMOTHER

You shiver to read
the death date
on a grave in June
where yolk-yellow buttercups
stir among briers
of unripe blackberries
as swallows twist
gobbling bluebottles
near a place where
a woman with cupped apron
once gathered eggs
died at thirty nine
and was they said
delicate as a dragonfly
and you forever unknown
to her look down
on a stone engraved
with the death date of one
the birth date of the other.

## STONES OF TIME

Sleepy with sun and wine
so good in the afternoon
as the breeze fills the sails

we float, glide
pierce the birth waters and he
blond and blue eyes to kill

holding a wet body
waiting for a breath hiss
waiting and watching

for years to come
staring skywards through lime foliage
to a black shadow

floating in arched movement
upward and outward
blood wet

at birth and death
I kiss a cold face
in the afternoon sun.

## COORDINATES

My son swaddled in sunflowers on a field in France,
wrapped around by a light halo in a glass-framed photo.

Through the window, a flash of pigeon-white
on sticky chestnut buds as an upstairs door opens.

I phone the clinic, ask for childhood records of mumps,
measles and rubella - needed for his leaving.

On his PC screen a dark Google map-line crosses America;
a red-haired girl looks out from *Facebook. She lost*

*her mother when she was ten,* he tells me,
*likes to collect old maps.* I face the space

beyond today, like turning my back
on the sun of a summer's evening.

# CRY OUT FOR THE DEAD

*Unstable Time*

## DURROW

And here's a plain of oak at Durrow
Where now the daffodils are thrown
To sounds of birdsong and mourners' sorrow.


The relic of a scribe who's trail of yellow
Twisted worm-like on a book in the gloom
Of a cell on an oak plain at Durrow.


And near Slighe Mor the standing stone
From where the prophet Cohn Cille
Set out for Iona and enduring sorrow.


A blond-haired youth looked down below
To watch his step fall through the air
Fall down and rest in a plain at Durrow.


And petals splash the oak with colour
Soon trampled flat with sacred clay
To sounds of birdsong and mourners' sorrow.


And silence trails the black night shadows
A silence rising to the moon
Broken by the wind on an oak plain at Durrow
That echoes with birdsong and mourners' sorrow.

## CONNECTED

My mother is dying tonight. I sit
on night-watch by her bed where she's wired

to a clicking syringe. I listen
to the hiss of flames from the stove

through the door and drink strong tea. I put
my hand on her head and threaded to her

wait for the cackle of dawn birds. I watch
the splashes of lemon light devour the dark

on a date they will carve in stone. I will look
in winter at her etched name smeared
with bird droppings.

*Patricia Byrne*

# DIES IRAE DIES ILLA

*Dies irae, dies illa*
Cry out in anger to the Lord
For the dead of the parish
Of Saint Margaret Mary Alacoque.

The people of Carrow, Cullintra and Derrymore
Cried out in anger for their dead
All waked and mourned and shouldered
To the church of Saint Margaret Mary Alacoque.

From the National School across the road
They came to sing at funeral masses
*Dies irae, dies illa*, they sang to groaning organ sounds
In the church of Saint Margaret Mary Alacoque.

Men sliced the sods of juicy peat
in the bogs of Tulrahan, Belleskar and Tawnamore
All now dead and mourned
In the church of Saint Margaret Mary Alacoque.

*Dies irae, dies illa*
Cry out in anger to the Lord
For the dead of the parish
Of Saint Margaret Mary Alacoque.

## MONTH'S MIND

It sits in a tin box
an *Aisling copybook*
*for pen and ink*
*in a class of its own*
on top of the oak wardrobe.


Starting from the back
she had ruled columns
listed names
ticked in red
those for her husband's memorial cards
ticked in blue
those for acknowledgements.


A roll call of the mourners
who one month ago
looked down on her body
in its best tweed suit.


Out the window
a crow picks holes
in the skin of
the autumn fruit.

## NO NIGHT

There is no night
No closing doors at dusk
No moving shapes on bog or water
No looking beyond the stars
No headlights funnelling paths on roads
No furtive creeping over boundary walls

There is no night
No crimson setting sun
No shadows prowling
No holy night, no silent night
No black awakening to thunder, wind and rain
No man in the moon laughing down at graves
No ghosts chasing fairies on Lios Ban hills

No dress rehearsal
For the tumble
Into blackness.

## DESCENT
*For grandfather*

You were a folklore figure
famous for the wild things you did
some said, a kind of Achilles.

You lifted a scythe to a crop of oats
cut a swathe the length of the field without stopping
some said, a powerful man.

You left a last indent of your head on a pillow
walked to work in Manchester
carrying a candle in your pocket.

You stepped into a crane bucket
to be winched forty feet below ground
where two men lay lifeless.

You were roped in the fireman's chair knot
your cloth cap abandoned
on a sewer shaft floor.

You came back in summer
when swallows skimmed waters at Riasc lake
and stooks of oats slanted in Lios Ban.

Four men held ropes tight
lowered you slowly
down.

*Patricia Byrne*

# ECHOES AND SILENCES

## TALES

Swans stop traffic at Westfields and waddle across the road.
A man shouts from a car window: *hurry up there swans.*

Friends speak of mothers: *Your one had no time for the mother - you
know. My mother - she was kind and genteel.*

Men fit a security alarm. One shouts instructions from a gate to
the other at an upstairs window. *Got you,* he calls down.

A son phones home and asks what he should get his girl for Valentine's.
*What about a bright bunch of flowers from Moore Street,* she suggests.

A couple meet at a pizza counter. He says, *I think I'd like to be married.*
She says, *I've been married three times. It's nothing to write home about.*

Two robins sit on a bare oak branch, turn their tails to me in the cream
light of a spring evening, eyeing each other.

## SCATTERY ISLAND

She kills time on the boat ride,
tidies her mobile address book,
selects contacts, names and options,
answers yes when asked *delete all details?*


She pushes buttons with no remorse at all,
wipes out Peter and Paul, removes Nellie,
discards Biljana, cuts out Ali and Ron.
In no time twenty identities are gone.


She lifts her head at Scarlet Reach and sees
a cormorant at The Dead Woman's Rock,
all black and silent. She knows this bird
will bide its time to pounce
at Owenogarney River mouth.


A shape looms ahead,
Scattery's round tower,
preserving patterns, prayers,
echoes and silences of the island.


She will obliterate no more.

## HY-BRAZIL
*Hy-Brazil is a mythical island supposedly seen off Achill every seven years and is likely a folk memory of submergence events on the island.*

Slievemore is black save for its tip.
The mountain looks down
on Krinnuck,
on Dugurt,
on me.

Waves swell and burst
at the back end of the island.
They spit milk-spray
on sheep,
on rocks,
on me.

A widening pool of light
glows
on Croaghaun,
on Dooagh,
on Dookinella.

Hy-Brazil, you float
in the western sky.
You raise me.

## CONVERSATION AT QUERRIN PIER

He's gathering bait at Querrin Pier
to fish for wrasse, he says, at The Arches of Ross.
I wait for the bloom of the flag iris
to start fishing for wrasse this time of the year.


I stay at the house near the shore
the one with the clump of ragged robin.
I moved back to the place I grew up in
when my wife died nine years ago now this year.


A curlew hangs straight up above us
its peaked bill ready to pounce.
I tell him it was tough to lose her so young
as he turns back to his bucket of bait.


The curlew hovers above
and waits
for us to be gone
on our ways.

# RESONANCE

The waves are quiet on Pollawaddy strand
at the end of the valley under Slievemore
quiet after the battering of last night's wind
the dawn a medley of black ground and trees
at the slopes of Krunnick.

I recall the story of the island woman
who married, moved inland, died young.
In the room with the chimney breast
she turned her face to the wall
and cried on her deathbed.

Was it a cry for
island waves
and gulls
and winds?

Sounds
like a tuning fork
vibrating
at a cave's
mouth.

## WEDDING DRESS
*At the Victorian Pier, Bangor, North Wales June 2009*

A sign on the pier reads:
'Shirley threw herself from this pier in 1997
in her wedding dress to raise funds for charity.
She died seven years later at the age of 44.'

Two seagulls make an exhibition flying above
the pier. They hover. One swoops down
like it might decapitate one.

A child waddles, trying to run a straight line
along the pier planks. Her mother rushes
in pursuit.

You think of Ann from Listowel, who lost her mother
the year of her First Communion. When she shopped
for her wedding dress, she buried her head in lace
and cried for the absent woman.

# BABBLE, MYTH AND FANTASY

*Unstable Time*

## ANECDOTAL


Her stories came from yarn and anecdote
Perspective was always her undoing
From babble, myth and fantasy she wrote.


A teller of tall tales how she could fabricate
With stoic stomach mix up everything
Her stories came from yarn and anecdote.


For she could spin fat yarns on things remote
Make myth, romance and fable of wrongdoing
From babble, myth and fantasy she wrote.


She knew dead writer words that she could quote
Bamboozle all with tricks of rhyme and writing
Her stories came from yarn and anecdote.


She'd babble on as in a bin of Beckett
Think she was author of *The Gathering*
From babble, myth and fantasy she wrote.


And in the end the words stuck in her throat
Perspective was always her undoing
Her stories came from yarn and anecdote
From babble, myth and fantasy she wrote.

## TAGINE

The lamb tagine is in the pot,
a shoulder-cut boned yesterday
on the butcher's bloodied block
then marinaded and seasoned
in mortared spice and tomato juice.
Now, onion, garlic and ginger blend
and brown in the pan while couscous
sharpens with lemon extract and mint.

Aromas float as I face the page,
prod words, mix nouns and verbs,
kill adjectives, catch images,
find turns, cut clichés, break lines.

The door bell rings. I fix my face,
shape my words and greet my guests.

## HEARING THINGS HERE
*On reading a newspaper report of Seamus Heaney's visit to*
*his old school at Anahorish, Count Derry in December 2007.*


My Granny English sold goats to your daddy,
the child tells him back at his old school.
My Granddad's daddy knew your cousin,
another pupil tells the Nobel Laureate.


They recite the parable of talents for him:
to everyone that has, more will be given.
The visitor is no hard man, reaping what was not sown
or gathering what was not scattered.


A girl stands and recites Anahorish,
speaks of the place where springs washed into grass
and lamps swung in yards as they went
to break ice at dunghills and wells.


This place is special to me too,
the poet tells them. This has to be one of the best
days yet. I'm hearing things here.


Behind the poet, a cameraman looks for an angle.

## ESSENTIAL WORK

My brother phones
when I'm on the island
staying at Dugort
under Slievemore.


On the radio people tell
how they heard the cry
of a mating fox
calling in the night wind
like a banshee.


My brother asks
what are you doing on the island?
I'm writing a poem, I reply.
Has to be done, I suppose, he says.

## SPOOFER

My love, my muse, my weaver of tall tales
How you can spin a yarn and fabricate
Make myths, romance, confuse *t's* and *th's*
In fantasies and fables you create.

I know that you can stay out of hot water
Bamboozle them with all the tricks you know
Deflate humbug that just will not hold water
My lover, trickster, fixer dynamo.

You shall be spoken of among northsiders
In Fagan's, Clonlife Road and All Hallows
And I will speak your name in my own thoughts
And woe begone all those who caused your woes.

And yes, my love, my muse, I have my joy
You are my spoofer, fibber lover boy.

## JACOB'S GIRLS
*June 2009*

Kimberley, Mikado and Coconut Creams
graced tea-tables for generations
and, not to be forgotten, the mysterious Fig Roll.
The Jacobs' Girls reminisce as they walk
through the Tallaght factory gates
for the last time.
'We hated the cerise pink overalls.
All the new girls had to wear them.'
A Jacob's girl is loyal to the end.
Asked: *How do they get the figs into the fig rolls?*
the answer is quick: *I'll take that secret
to the grave.*

# TOUCHED IN THE HEAD

## SAVIOUR BIRD

A goldfinch streaks across the kitchen window
foraging for shelter from the May hailstones.
The phone rings.

I'm calling from the hospital,
the consultant is meeting with his colleagues,
they think you're an interesting case.
Can you come in for review?

The rain swirls as if from a smoker's pipe.
It sluices the roof, cascades through gutters.
Already, I know what I'll say,
that I won't put up with their stares,
looking down on me as if
it's already the end.

The saviour bird twitters
knowingly
from the hedge
of thorns.

## TOUCHED IN THE HEAD
*Heat Wave in New York, Summer 2006*


The Empire State and Chrysler buildings
lower their lights as Mayor Bloomberg
hits the dimmer switch at a temperature
of 105 degrees Fahrenheit on a day
when Baghdad Architect Zaha Hadid
exhibits at The Guggenheim. Fluid fields
of ruptured lines withstand chaos.
Shapes evolve image by image
and zigzag in mid air. Bellies
of translucent glass with playful geometries
give form to space — a frozen moment pulled taut,
snaps and splinters as the point of support
disappears like a necklace disintegrating.
Skyscrapers turn on their sides,
vast spaces are sliced, frozen in motion.
Layered spaces of brutal concrete
tilt and move and all appears ruptured.
Castro has stomach surgery and
endangered turtles die in Lebanon
as flaming oil sends waves of smoke
to the heavens. New York is touched
in the head, like it's gone
off its rocker
again.

## ALL EYES

I stop for coffee
at the motel near Galway
on my way west when I see a woman
with a takeaway cup of latte in the ladies
struggling to open the cubicle door with her latte-less
hand and seeing only the back of her head
I'm not able to look her straight
in the eye that day in
Oranmore.

Leaving that place
I have forgotten the code for
the car-park barrier when a watching
ginger-haired man calls out let's try all the fives
and the barrier lifts as he shouts at me to get out quick or
it will come down and kill you stone dead
and he laughs as I leave and when
I move out onto the road he
keeps an eye out.

## STAY AWAY FROM BEING ORDINARY

Mighty, he said, mighty
an incredible trilogy
a four hour epic of beauty
a whirlwind start
showing massive hunger
wand-weaving magicians
annex our imaginations
like usurpers in a Mafia turf war
not choked by history
or gazing at legends
dark and peevish
playing at one hundred per cent
no benchmark for their expectations
in a world where grubby merchants rule
this is too great a story for detractors
this day will see great heroism flowering
as they bend to hypnotic rhythms
finish the ascent, plant the flag
shattered after exertions
like the final reel of a blockbuster
stay away from being ordinary
enjoy the beautiful journey
go to sleep dreaming.

*Patricia Byrne*

## A HALF DOZEN

We've six of them
four boys and two girls
took them to Portugal
all six of them
threw everything into the bags
did the ironing over there
we all need a break
feeding them is the worst of it
I boil a dozen eggs every morning
let them eat them for breakfast
or throw them into sandwiches
for lunch
for the six of them
keeps the hunger at bay I say
they love Christmas cake
all six of them
so I make it all year round
I've pounds of fruit steeping
in there right now
as for himself, he's OK
he'd sweep the floor all day
but never think of washing it
that sort — you know yourself
but we wouldn't be without them
all six of them
we love them to death.

## QUINCENTENNIAL BRIDGE

Learner writers hear of twisted apples and stare
at Quincentennial Bridge,
heads filled with odds and ends of things as eyes hover
on Quincentennial Bridge.

The Donegal poet speaks of cats, crows and Kafka
and poems coming anytime, anywhere as they drive in September
over Quincentennial Bridge.

Gulls float above in their otherworldliness, like they're licking
Heaven and a rat crawls on broken glass at the flyover base
of Quincentennial Bridge.

A man in blue shirt sleeves looks at the road ahead, and Kerouac's words
explode in his mind, like spiders, on the walkover
of Quincentennial Bridge.

The otter woman approaches, and crosses the confluence
of sea and river, mourning, on the night of the full moon, over
on Quincentennial Bridge.

This, Byrne, is not the place for recuperation, for resting
on your laurels, for you will graduate from here and move far away
from Quincentennial Bridge.

# UNSTABLE TIME

## OUT OF SEQUENCE

Last night, my second-born said,
last night I was awake
for a long time.
And when I did sleep,
he said,
I dreamt there was a number missing.


On our last day at school,
he said,
when we all stood together for the school photo
Peter whispered *Now lads, when I say the word*
*I want you all to move together*
*and drive your man crazy.*


They moved together,
all together that last day
in perfect unison,
not knowing that on another day
one among them would jump
alone through the air.


Now, I'm afraid to sleep,
my second-born said.
I'm afraid of that number
going round and round
in my head
out of sequence like
last night.

## MOTHER'S DAY

Buses disgorge visitors at the gates.
Crowds move along two paths,
herded by their guides. A child cries
'Mama, wait for me.'


The poplars rock in white packed snow,
catkins drop like caterpillars
to ash-rich earth. Branches taper
to the sky in prayer.


A text message from home: *miss you Mum,
wish you were here for lunch
on Mother's Day.*


Coots glide on nearby waters.
A car cracks
to life.


What did those poplars see and hear?

## WHEELING AWAY

They cycle in tandem
through Querrin, Doonaha,
Carrigaholt and Kilkee,
she and he.

An old woman shouted
*it's the best way to travel*
and stooped to pick foxglove
as they pass
she and he.

They cycle in tandem
look down on the ocean,
stop pedalling,
change gear
and free wheel
she and he.

And soon
dusk is falling.
He asks
*is there time?*
She answers
*time up*
*wheel*
*away.*

CROSSING

I read a strange thing today:
that you have one hour
to select one memory
to take with you —
all others memories will cease to exist.


Days before she died my mother said:
Do you know what I like to remember?
What? I ask.
I like to remember how we ran
as children in the fields at Gurteen
and jumped the bog-holes
and laughed as we crossed.


And this is the memory I select —
a woman's laughter
as she crosses
from this place
to the next.

## MOMENTS

In a field
of ripened oats where a rabbit escapes through
a gorse hedge on an August afternoon.

At a school wall
chin on rough stone, watching newly-weds emerge
from the church of Saint Margaret Mary Alacoque.

In a dormitory
surrounded by sterile calico curtains
in the month John F Kennedy was shot.

In the Catskill Mountains
shocked by the sheets of heat and skunk smells
in the early morning air.

In a maternity ward
frightened by pain, unable to sleep, listening
to night-traffic on Limerick's Ennis Road.

At a bed-side
where a body falls sideways, a tongue slips from
a mouth and death is viewed head-on.

On a page
pencil marks delineate life moments as the light
of a May morning lingers on a writer's fingers.

## UNSTABLE TIME

*Inspired by Michael Minnis' DVD projection 'Sunrise over
The Dnzpro River' at Limerick City Gallery, October 2007.*

Frame I

I know this dawn scene is not a still
when an insect crawls across the screen
and pixels move at the edges of trees.
Layers of grey and taupe on water and sky.
Lemon light pushes from the east,
as if through stained glass.
Early morning figures move on-screen
and a silhouette walks towards me
in unstable time.

Frame II

I will turn my back on this shifting dawn,
walk to the butcher's, buy a shoulder of lamb,
braise it for hours this Saturday afternoon
when time slowly inches. We will eat together,
switch channels between soccer and rugby,
two games at the one time,
while we are here,
now,
nowhere else.

*Patricia Byrne*